Mutterings of An Earthling

Aireena Ab Karim

BookLeaf Publishing

Presentation by *BookLeaf Publishing*

Web: www.bookleafpub.com

E-mail: info@bookleafpub.com

ISBN: 9789357212458

First edition 2023

ACKNOWLEDGEMENT

I would like to say my thanks and praise to God Almighty for allowing me the chance to write these poems.
I would like to thank my husband, my family and my friends.
Thank you.

Dear Dad

Dad
You're such an inspiration
You're full of dedication

You sacrificed your whole life
To give your family a good life

You are dear to your patients
You treat our family with love and kindness

It's hard to be in your shoes
I could never reach your heights
Whatever decision I choose
It will never be right

Long after your passing
Your legacy is still everlasting
May you rest in peace
And be showered be blessings

Hesitation

I missed out on a good deed today
Cause I hesitated

A lady at the cash register
Had forgotten her wallet
I could have helped her
But I paused and kept quiet

As I drove back home, I couldn't stop thinking
I wished I had offered her help
Instead of sitting here just wishing

Doing good is food for your soul
So next time, i will no longer hesitate
And just go for it!

Emotions

Sunny and bright outside
Too bad sometimes that's not what we're feeling inside
That's how humans are
All our emotions we like to hide

Well, sometimes our life is not always full of colour
But we can try to make it a less duller

Whether its storms or whatever the weather
Try to look at the brighter picture

Let us stop worrying and be grateful
Because life is too short to just dwell and be sorrowful

What they say

You're a disappointment
You're an embarrassment
You lack any passion
That's what they said

You should do better
You should aim higher
You should put your act together
That's what they said

But remember,
It does not matter
How people define you
Because only you know yourself
So just be beautiful YOU

Rise back

Life has its ups and downs
We can always rise back after we fall down

Even if life stop you in its tracks
You can always bounce back

Why people hurt others

People will bruise you
Cause they themselves are bruised
People will hurt you
Cause they themselves are hurt

Be it intentionally or unintentionally
There will be times you get offended easily
And times when you get over it wholeheartedly

When they say hurtful things
Try to pause and think
Is it true what they're saying
Or it does not hold any meaning

Do not let it define you
And don't let it consume you
Rise above and let it go
Be the better person and continue to grow

To forgive

Learning to forgive
It's not easy at it seems

Forgiveness is not for them
But it is for you
For you to blossom and be a new you

Forgiveness heals and mends your soul
Your soul needs this healing
For you to be whole

Forgiving is for your peace of mind
And for you to move forward
You don't know the storms in their minds
So let it slide and pay it forward

Roadblocks

There are roadblocks of life
We may stumble upon
But we shall strive
And continue head on

As we get stuck
Or feel out of luck
Go and explore
Do things you never do before

A change of scene
A breath of fresh air
Reminisce where you've been
And come back with a new flair

All over again

You fell in love all over again
As you lay eyes on your little one

The small feet and small hands
You cherish them as they fit perfectly in your
hands

That newborn scent
A distinctive smell
All your worries went
It's like being struck with a spell

I love you my little baby
With all of my heart
May you grow strong and healthy
Be in this world to play a part

A secret

Do you want to know a secret
To living a life without resentment

It is to stop comparing
And to own a little less
Ponder on your blessings
And look at those who have much less

Enjoy every single moments
And say your thanks
For the key to happiness
Is to live life full of gratefulness

My superpower

What is self-empowerment?
Is it a list of perfect resumes, or high-end achievements?

No. It is knowing your self-worth
And finding your passion
And to put in efforts for self-compassion

So, block out your fears
Reach out for your targets
Your goals matter
However long it might take

You see, self-empowerment is like a superpower
It's the best feeling when we can help each other
As empowered people will empower another

Mindfulness

Our minds in a whirlwind
Our bodies in autopilot
How can we learn to unwind
And not live like a robot

It is to be mindful
And self-aware
Take time to be grateful
And stare at the nature out there

Be in tune with your breathing
Put your focus in that moment
Let go of whatever is happening
And try to live in that very moment

Mindfulness is the way
For your mind to break free
Put those worries at bay
Declutter your mind and set it free

Missing out

As you watch others graduate
And climbed that staircase of success
You can't help but think
Why I haven't reached that yet

Maybe my success has yet to come
Or it may be in different shape or form
Be patient my dear, your time will come

Life is beautiful

Do things that make your heart full
And surely you will see this life is truly beautiful

This little thing

There's this little thing in our brain
It's called Amygdala
It makes our body go fight or flight, or curl like
a koala

But aside from that,
Have you heard of an 'Amygdala Hijack'?
It's something that can cause us to overreact
Or do some actions we might later regret

See, your thoughts, emotions and behaviours
Are interconnected to one another

Each time we feel like we're attacked
Do some self-regulation
And we can try this mind-hack

Pause, take deep breaths and observe those
thoughts
Observe without judgements for 90 seconds

And then let it pass, and let it float
So, there you go, as easy as that
You can try it as an antidote

We are humans

We are humans, not angels
That are created without flaws
So be kind to each other and try to overlook the flaws

Lessons

Be thankful for the lessons
Indeed, there is lessons to learn in every
situation

Finding peace

As you go through life
As you go through this world
Tests and trials are so rife
Having patience is a pearl

You turn for help towards the creation
But all the creations are having soul starvation

So, you turn towards the Creator
As you know, He is your Sustainer
He told us to seek help with patience and prayer

Then you find your heart is at ease
As He said it twice, surely with every hardship
there is ease
With every hardship there is ease

And truly in the remembrance of God, do hearts
find peace

www.ingramcontent.com/pod-product-compliance
Lightning Source LLC
Chambersburg PA
CBHW051723130826
49812CB00034B/1312
9789357212458

Man-To-Man Talk

ILYA BLOYE

BookLeaf Publishing

Presentation by *BookLeaf Publishing*

Web: www.bookleafpub.com

E-mail: info@bookleafpub.com

ISBN: 9789357214117

First edition 2023

My First December Poem

Twas a misty time, on a Monday morning
A man stood, for he was mourning
A loss on Christmas Eve, a friend...
God, make this dam war end!

My Second December Poem

A new generation,
They look at the screen.
They ignore all they hear,
And don't want to be seen.

My Third December Poem

The money in his pocket,
It jingles, jangles, jingles.
The lad down the road
Just bought a pack'o pringles.

My Fourth December Poem

World leaders sit at a table,
A map of the world lays in front of them.
They play their twisted game of soldiers,
Who cares who lives and who dies?...

My Fifth December Poem

The world keeps on spinning,
And a lot of us are fine.
But even if it's not,
It's a great thing, Life!

My Sixth December Poem

The wind whistled loudly,
And the rain pored heavily.
A man stood there and said:
"Ah, a good English day! Lovely"

My Seventh December Poem

A piano trainee plays the instrument,
Plank, plink, plank.
The trainer sighs and shakes his head,
Plank, plink, plank.

My Eighth December Poem

Europeans speak gobble de goop,
And its the same for the globe.
So no wonder it's a common question:
Why do different languages exist?

My Ninth December Poem

Pasta and pizza,
They're such yummy pleasures.
But, as all things in life,
They are greater in measures.

My Tenth December Poem

The teen sits at a PC,
The adult at a TV.
No-one ever seems to have time,
Nor for pets, nor for tea.

My Eleventh December Poem

A man sat in a rocking chair,
He rocked to and fro,
Oh, he had seen so many things,
From being called "Sir",
to being called "Bro".

My Twelfth December Poem

I love water, and I'll tell you why,
I'll explain it so much it might make you cry,
But the taste is so simple, so empty, so plain,
That I love it enough even to drink it on a plane.

My Thirteenth December Poem

It's snowing, it's snowing, it's snowing,
Its snowing enough for a pie.
It's snowing, it's snowing, it's snowing,
Alright, that's enough, goodbye.

My Fourteenth December Poem

A boy sat in bed, phone in hand,
Playing games that brought him pleasure,
And thought to himself, whilst sipping warm tea,
"Ah, a great thing, leisure."

My Fifteenth December Poem

The man looked out the window,
And felt a great joy,
And memories came back,
Of parties and toys,
So it just goes to show, big or small,
Christmas is a time loved by all!

My Sixteenth December Poem

The music roared through the hall,
And people played Hip Hop and other malarky,
And in this giant mess of celebration,
People really know how to party!

My Seventeenth December Poem

Dogs, they come in varying shapes and sizes,
In many breeds, colours and different colour
eyes,
But what a pet dog truly needs,
Is a heart and soul the size of a pine tree.

My Eighteenth December Poem

The ice thawed and cracked away,
The snow evaporates and melts.
A farmer might cheer, a student might gloom,
But that's England for you, me mates.

My Nineteenth December Poem

Are there miracles?... Good question,
For any Aristotles out there,
The answer could be bitter,
Or as delicious as a pear.
For miracles can happen just like that,
Or only when you're out in Costa,
But, as the Russians may put it,
"А это, друг, не так-то просто."

My Twentieth December Poem

A Christmas Carol is one of the best,
Ask Dave, ask Bob, ask Pickens.
And people might even after many centuries, say
"Good Job, Dickens!"

My Twenty-First December Poem

Christmas! A time of cheer,
Of gifting, of loving, of supporting all,
So maybe, just maybe, I can get away with
rhyming this with "all":
Merry Christmas, one and all!

www.ingramcontent.com/pod-product-compliance
Lightning Source LLC
Chambersburg PA
CBHW051723130826
49812CB00034B/1311
* 9 7 8 9 3 5 7 2 1 4 1 1 7 *